# The City-States in Ancient Greece

## Government Books for Kids

## Children's Government Books

**BABY PROFESSOR**

EDUCATION KIDS

Speedy Publishing LLC

40 E. Main St. #1156

Newark, DE 19711

www.speedypublishing.com

Copyright 2017

Ancient Greece wasn't always a single country or an empire united under its single government, it consisted of several city-states.

A powerful city would be located at each city-state's center. The city then ruled the area and lands that surrounded it.

This city would also sometimes rule over smaller, less-powerful cities. The Greek word for city-state is "polis".

Each polis would have its separate government. Some city states were known as monarchies that were ruled by tyrants or kings.

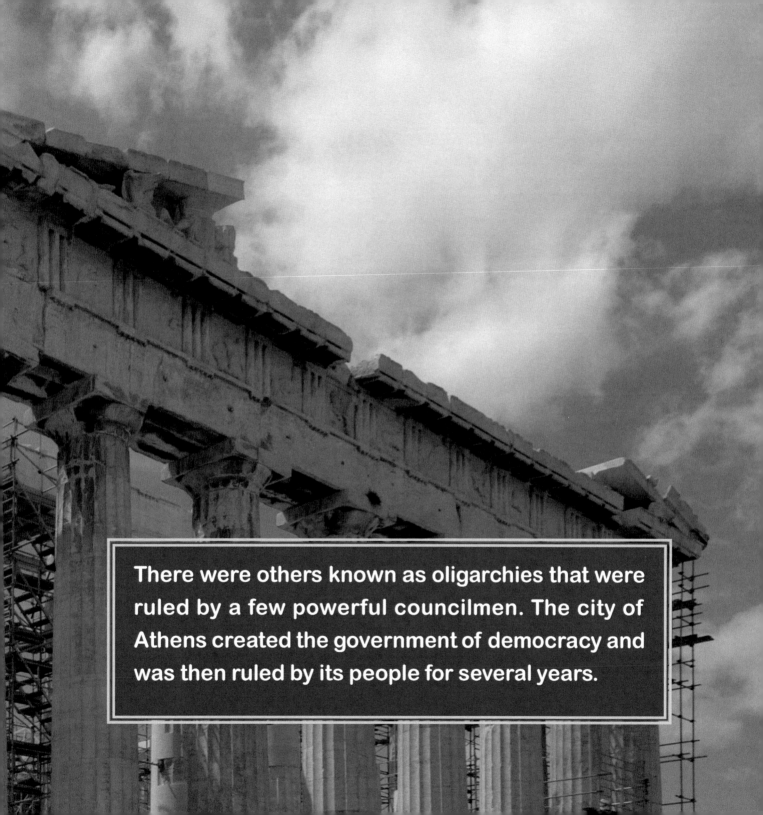

There were others known as oligarchies that were ruled by a few powerful councilmen. The city of Athens created the government of democracy and was then ruled by its people for several years.

People that lived in Ancient Greece did not considered themselves to be "Greek", but considered themselves to be citizens of their city-state.

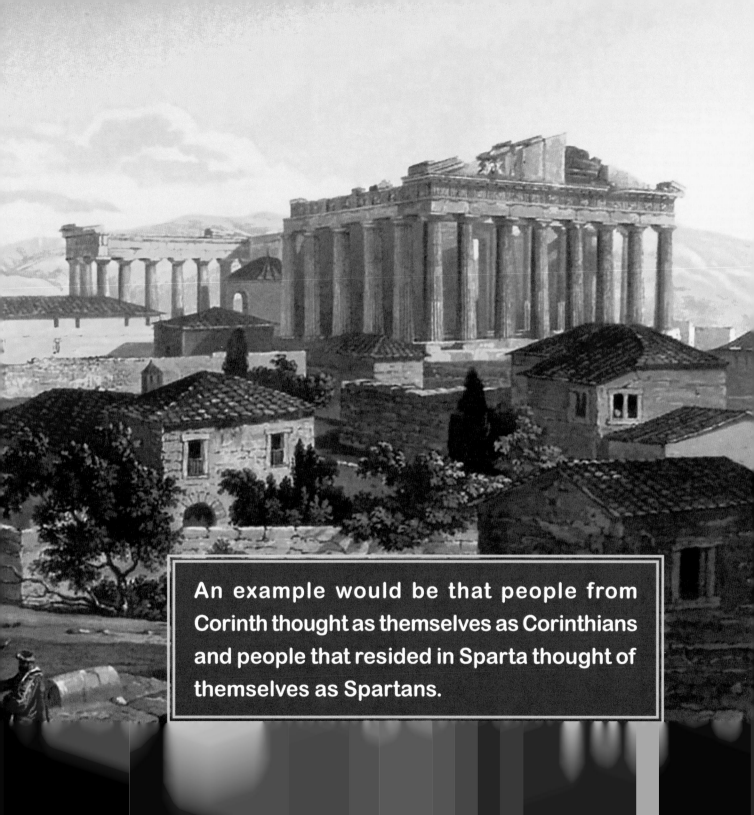

An example would be that people from Corinth thought as themselves as Corinthians and people that resided in Sparta thought of themselves as Spartans.

Rhodes, Corinth, and Thebes, among others, played an important role during the time of the Roman Empire.

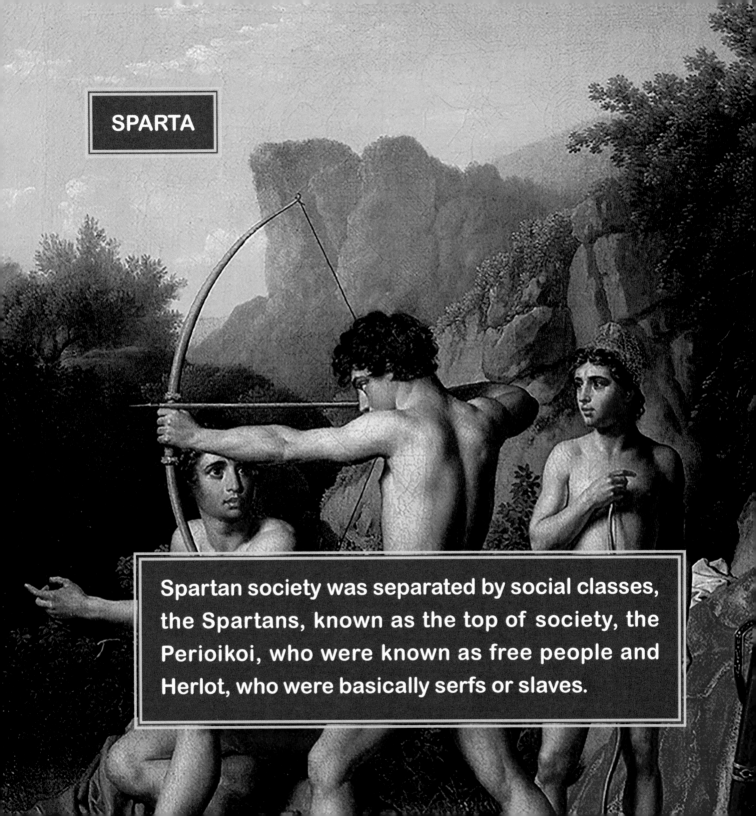

**SPARTA**

Spartan society was separated by social classes, the Spartans, known as the top of society, the Perioikoi, who were known as free people and Herlot, who were basically serfs or slaves.

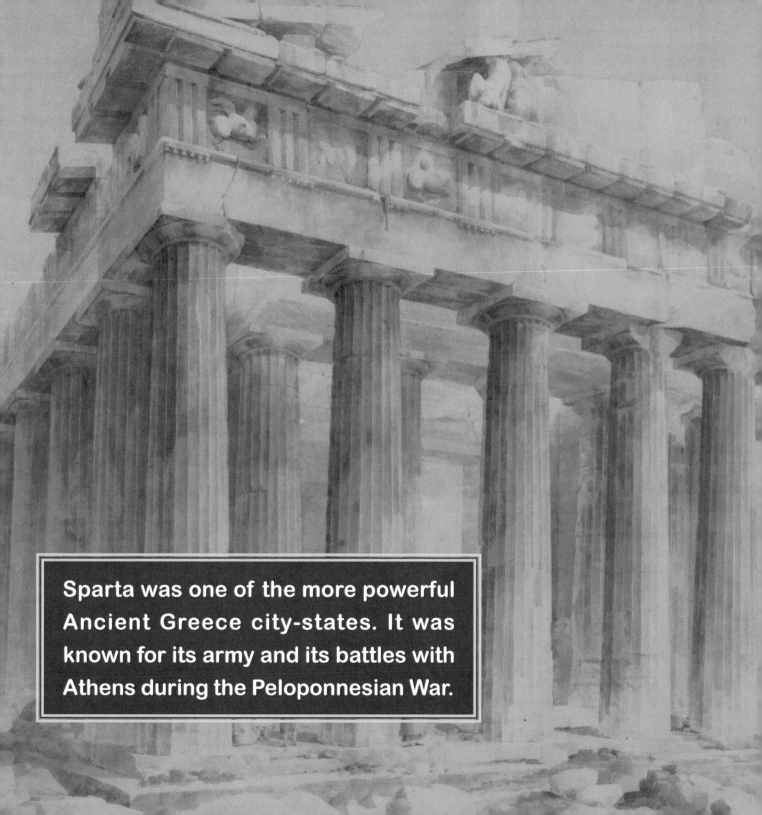

Sparta was one of the more powerful Ancient Greece city-states. It was known for its army and its battles with Athens during the Peloponnesian War.

It was located on the banks of the Eurotas River in a southeast corner of Greece. Messenia and Laconia were the lands that it had control over.

The boys would be trained at a young age to be soldiers. Their mothers would raise them until they turned seven and they would then be sent to the Agoge, a military school.

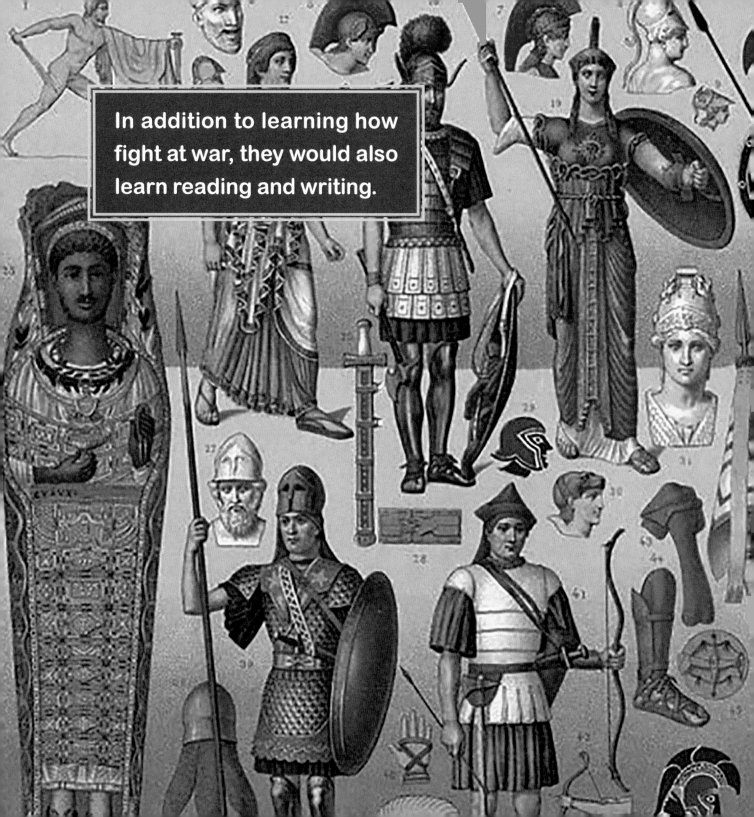

In addition to learning how fight at war, they would also learn reading and writing.

Spartan's Army would fight in what was known as the Phalanx formation. This consisted of lining up next to each other.

Then they would advance by locking their shields and stabbing the enemy with spears. They spent their life practicing this formation and you could see this in the way they fought their battles. They would rarely break this formation which made it possible for them to win over armies of greater sizes.

Spartan gained power approximately 650 BC. Beginning in 492 BC through 449 BC, the Spartans would lead in a war versus the Persians. It was during these wars that they fought the well-known Battle of Thermopylae. They allowed the Greek army to escape as 300 Spartans were able to hold off thousands of Persians.

During the Peloponnesian War, Sparta fought Athens. This lasted from 431 to 404 BC and eventually Sparta was triumphant over Athens. It began to decline and then lost to Thebes in 371 BC during the Battle of Leuctra. It did, however, remain independent until the Roman Empire conquered Greece in 146 BC.

ATHENS

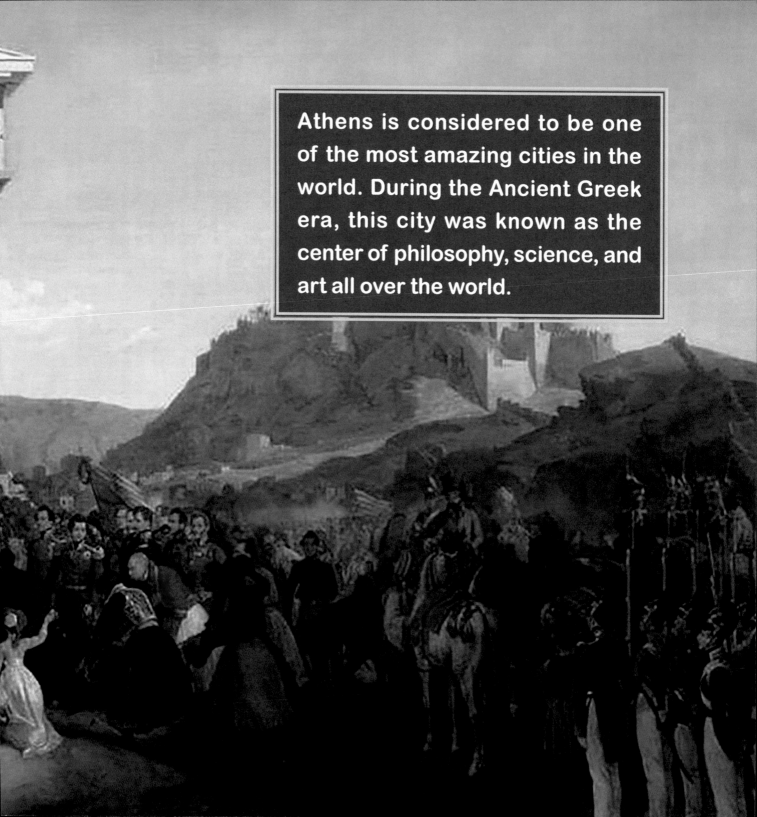

Athens is considered to be one of the most amazing cities in the world. During the Ancient Greek era, this city was known as the center of philosophy, science, and art all over the world.

Athens' history dates back more than 3400 years, making it one of the oldest cities. It is known to be the birthplace of democracy and considered the heart of the civilization of Ancient Greece.

Athens was named for Athena, a Greek goddess. She was known as the goddess of civilization, war, and wisdom, and was the patron for that city. The Parthenon, her shrine, is on a hill located at the middle of Athens.

The agora was known to be the center of government and commerce for Athens. It consisted of an open area which was used for meetings and was encircled by buildings. Several of these buildings were built as temples, including those built to Apollo, Hephaestus, and Zeus.

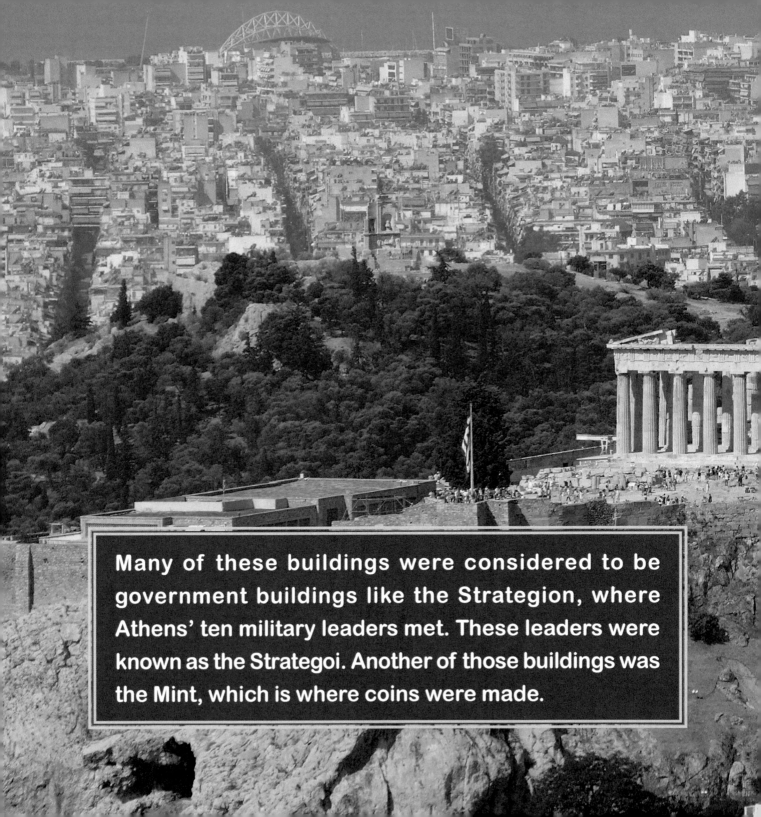

Many of these buildings were considered to be government buildings like the Strategion, where Athens' ten military leaders met. These leaders were known as the Strategoi. Another of those buildings was the Mint, which is where coins were made.

People would meet at the agora to discuss government and philosophy ideals. This is where democracy came to life for ancient Greece.

In the middle of the city, on a hill, was the Acropolis. It was surrounded by walls made of stone and originally was built to be a fortress and citadel.

This is where people could go if it came under attack. Many buildings and temples followed overlooking the city.

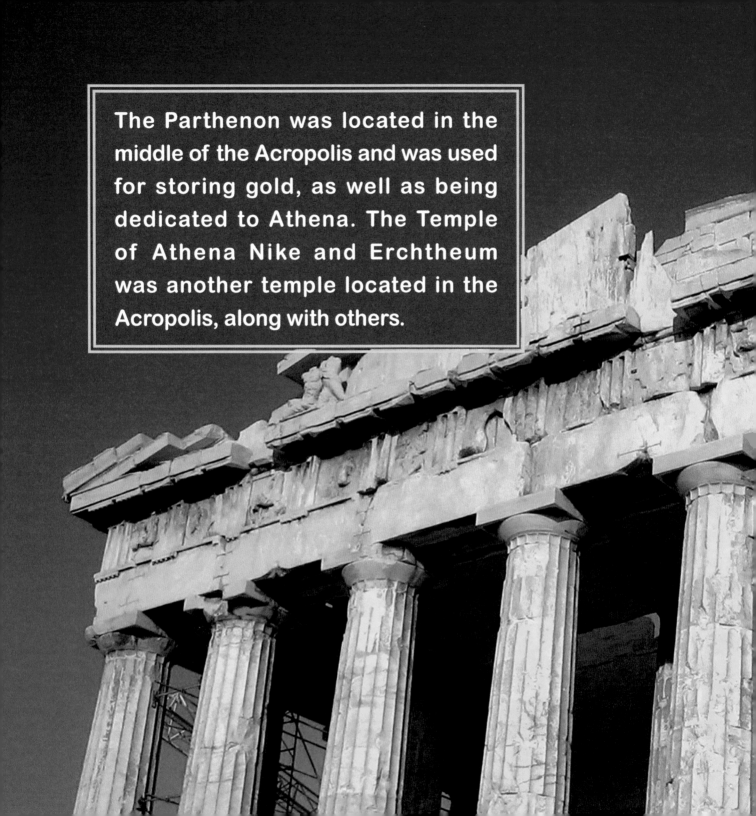

The Parthenon was located in the middle of the Acropolis and was used for storing gold, as well as being dedicated to Athena. The Temple of Athena Nike and Erchtheum was another temple located in the Acropolis, along with others.

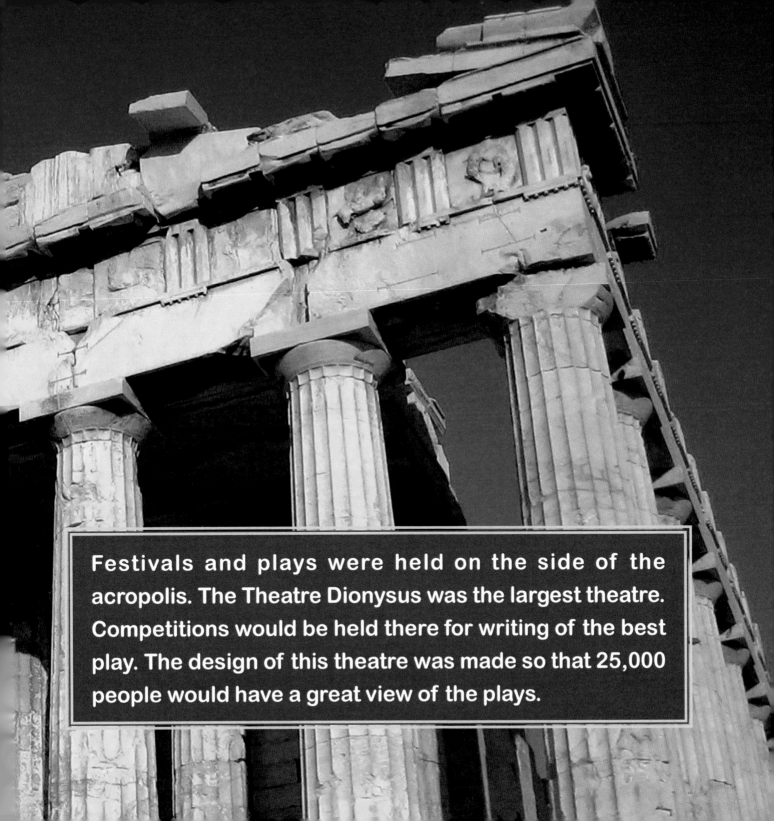

Festivals and plays were held on the side of the acropolis. The Theatre Dionysus was the largest theatre. Competitions would be held there for writing of the best play. The design of this theatre was made so that 25,000 people would have a great view of the plays.

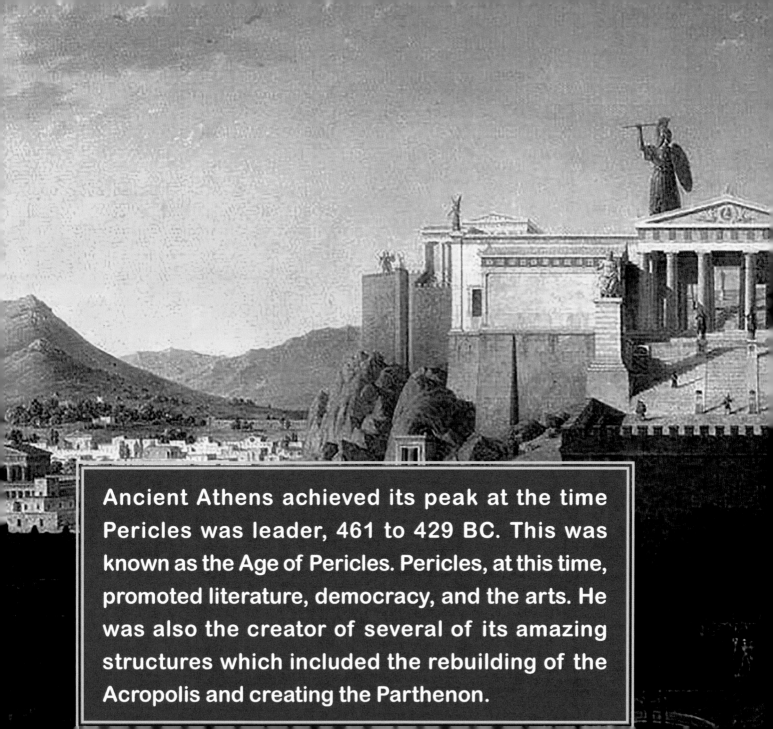

Ancient Athens achieved its peak at the time Pericles was leader, 461 to 429 BC. This was known as the Age of Pericles. Pericles, at this time, promoted literature, democracy, and the arts. He was also the creator of several of its amazing structures which included the rebuilding of the Acropolis and creating the Parthenon.

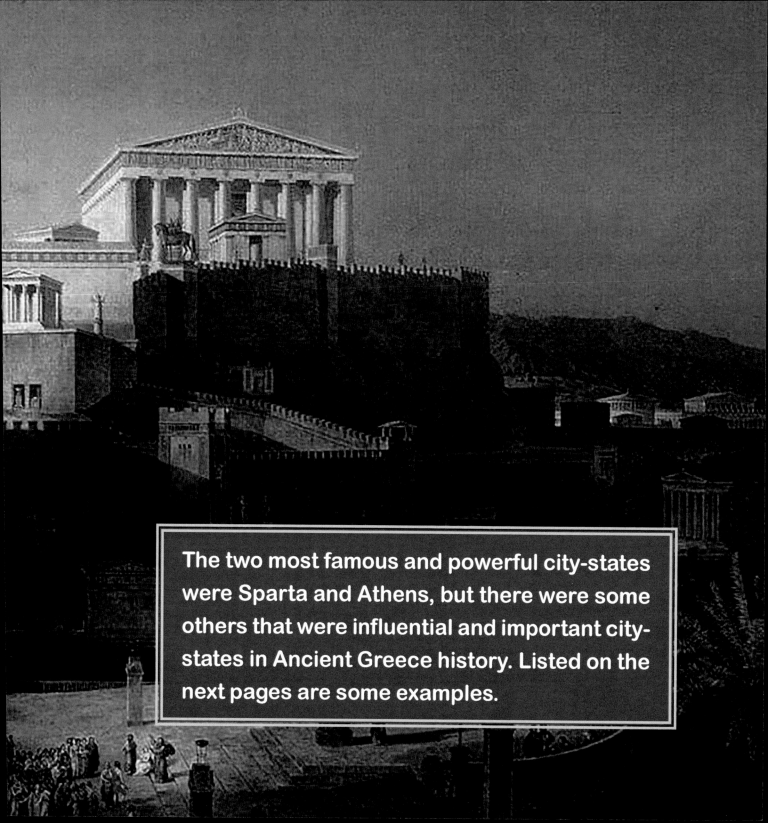

The two most famous and powerful city-states were Sparta and Athens, but there were some others that were influential and important city-states in Ancient Greece history. Listed on the next pages are some examples.

CORINTH

Corinth was in a great location and was considered a trade city. This allowed there to be two seaports, one on the Corinthian Gulf and another on the Saronic Gulf. Because of this, it become known as one of the wealthier cities of Ancient Greece.

They created their own coinage and required traders to use these coins if they were in their city.

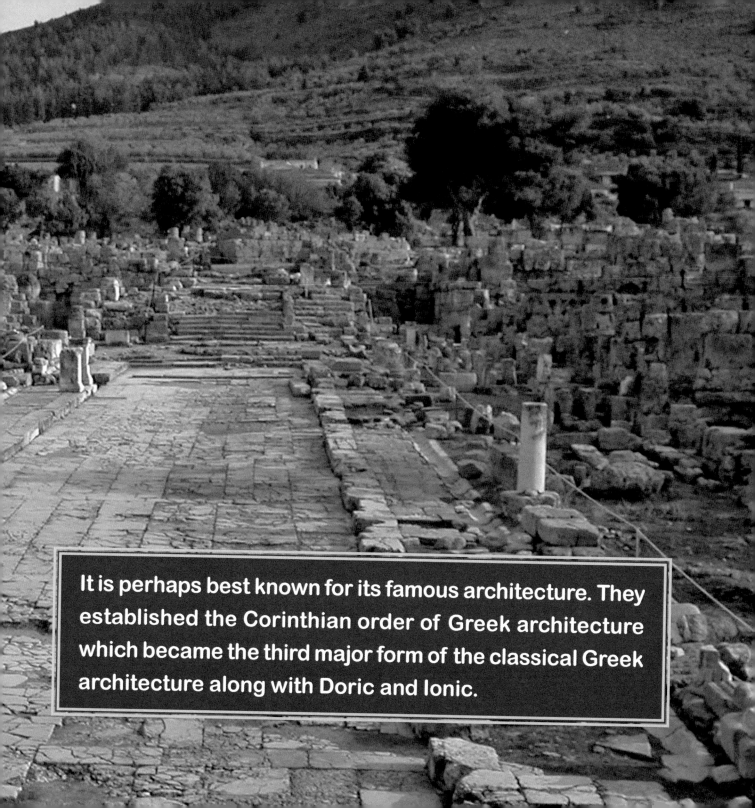

It is perhaps best known for its famous architecture. They established the Corinthian order of Greek architecture which became the third major form of the classical Greek architecture along with Doric and Ionic.

They were considered a monarchy which was ruled by a king. During the Persian Wars, they would provide soldiers to the Greeks. They also united against Athens, with Sparta, during the Peloponnesian War.

# THEBES

Thebes was known as a powerful city-state north of Athens and Corinth that was always switching sides during the many Greek wars.

It was at the time of the Persian Wars that they sent soldiers to Thermopylae to fight against the Persians, but then later, they connected with King Xerxes I of Persia to fight Athens and Sparta.

They would ally with Athens against Sparta during different times and would then switch sides to partner with Sparta against Athens.

Thebes, in 371 BC, marched in opposition to Sparta which led to defeat of the Spartans. This was known as the Battle of Leuctra. This ended the power of the city-state of Sparta and several of the Spartan slaves were set free.

Thebes was also well respected in Greek literature and legend too. It was the birthplace of Hercules, the Greek hero, and also played a giant role in the legends of Dionysus and Oedipus. Pinda, who was possibly the famous Greek poet at that time, also lived there.

**ARGOS**

Argo first became known as a power under Pheidon during 7th century BC. During his reign, Argos introduced the silver coins and a system of measures and weights that became known as the Pheidonian measures.

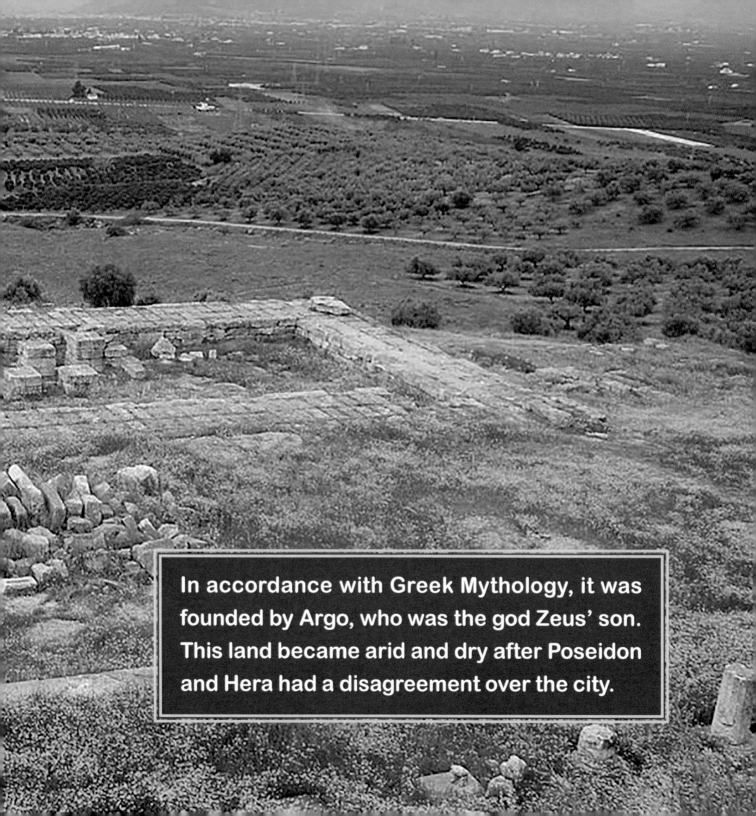

In accordance with Greek Mythology, it was founded by Argo, who was the god Zeus' son. This land became arid and dry after Poseidon and Hera had a disagreement over the city.

Hera defeated Poseidon and became patron of this city, but Poseidon then was able to get revenge by drying the land out.

Delphi was known as the spiritual center. People would come from near and far to visit its city and receive leadership from the Delphic oracle Pythia. During this classical time, it became shrine to Apollo once he killed Python.

DELPHI

It was also the center for arts, trade, literature, and education. Since its location was at the center of Greece, it was referred to the "navel (center) of the world". It also was home of the Pythian Games, a well-known athletic competition held in the early times of Greece.

RHODES

Rhodes was created in 408 BC on an island in Greece when three cities known as Lindosk, Kamiros, and Lalyssos made the decision to unite into one larger city. It did well for many years because it was a great location for a port.

It was also known for the shipbuilders and for a giant statue they named Colossus of Rhodes.

This statute was considered to be one of the Seven Ancient Wonders of the World. It represented the Greek Titan Helios and was over 100 feet tall.

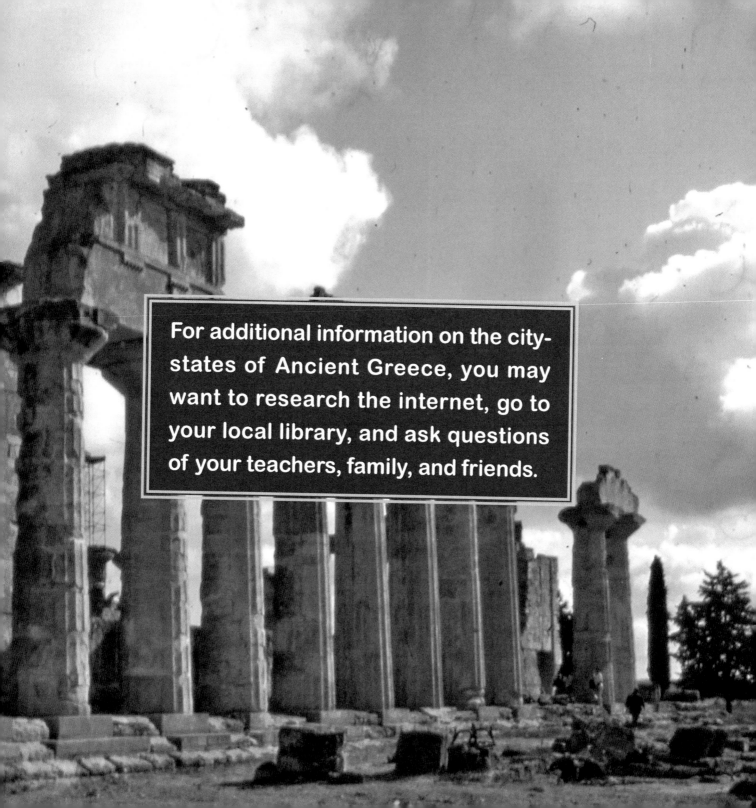

For additional information on the city-states of Ancient Greece, you may want to research the internet, go to your local library, and ask questions of your teachers, family, and friends.

Visit

BABY PROFESSOR
EDUCATION KIDS

www.BabyProfessorBooks.com

to download Free Baby Professor eBooks and view
our catalog of new and exciting Children's Books

57001477R00038

Made in the USA
Middletown, DE
26 July 2019